Beethoven
FOR BEGINNING PIANO SOLO

T0087309

ON THE COVER:
Wanderer above the Sea of Fog (1818)
by Caspar David Friedrich (1774–1840)

ISBN 978-1-5400-8890-1

Copyright © 2020 by HAL LEONARD LLC
International Copyright Secured All Rights Reserved

Visit Hal Leonard Online at
www.halleonard.com

Contact us:
Hal Leonard
7777 West Bluemound Road
Milwaukee, WI 53213
Email: info@halleonard.com

In Europe, contact:
Hal Leonard Europe Limited
42 Wigmore Street
Marylebone, London, W1U 2RN
Email: info@halleonardeurope.com

In Australia, contact:
Hal Leonard Australia Pty. Ltd.
4 Lentara Court
Cheltenham, Victoria, 3192 Australia
Email: info@halleonard.com.au

ECOSSAISE IN G MAJOR

By LUDWIG VAN BEETHOVEN

Allegretto

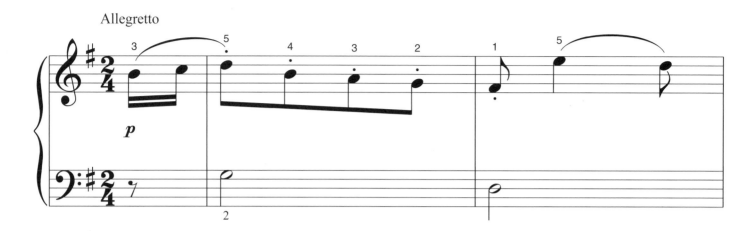

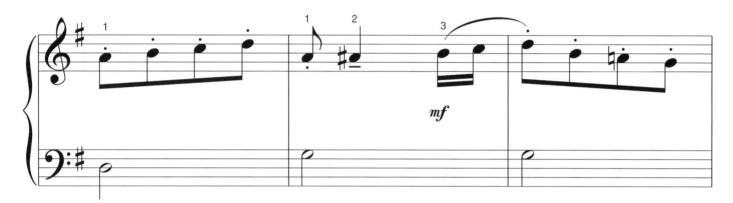

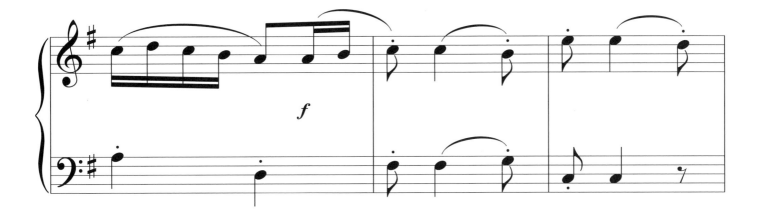

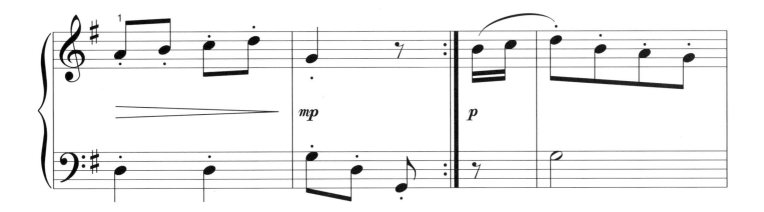

FÜR ELISE

By LUDWIG VAN BEETHOVEN

Flowing

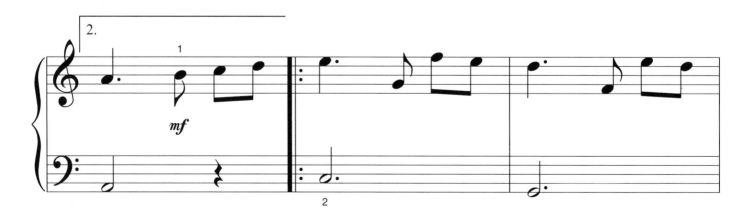

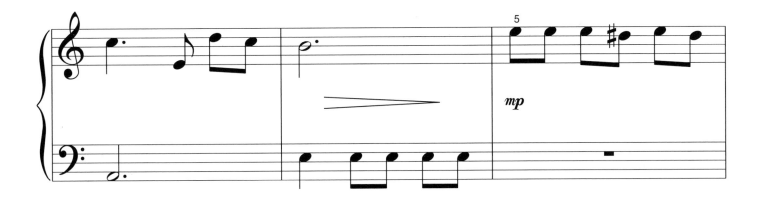

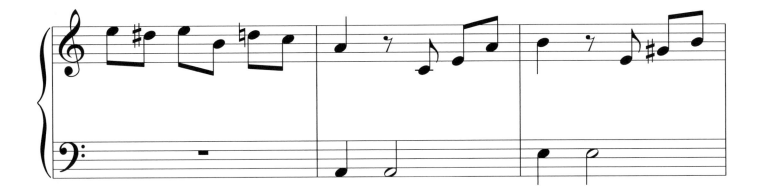

MINUET IN G MAJOR

By LUDWIG VAN BEETHOVEN

Allegretto

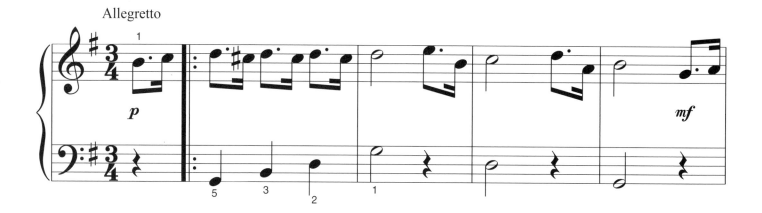

ODE TO JOY

from SYMPHONY NO. 9 in D Minor, Fourth Movement Choral Theme

By LUDWIG VAN BEETHOVEN

Majestically

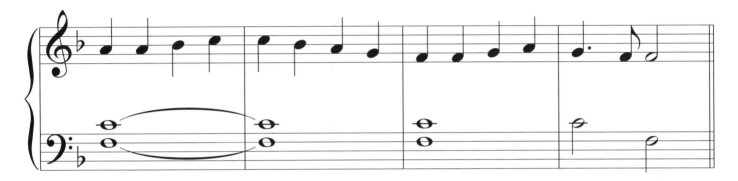

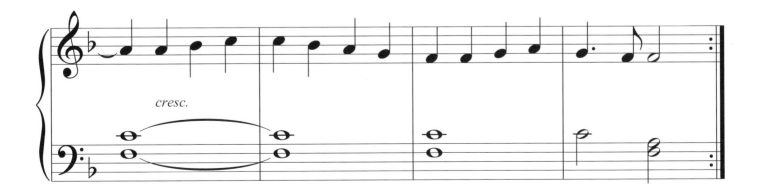

"MOONLIGHT" SONATA
First Movement Theme

By LUDWIG VAN BEETHOVEN

Adagio

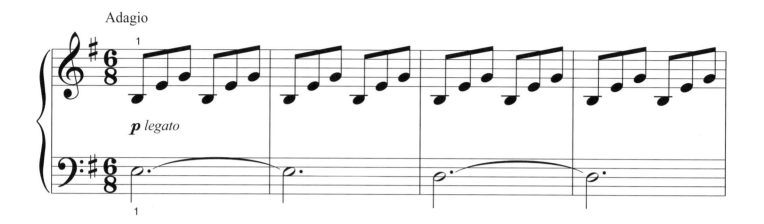

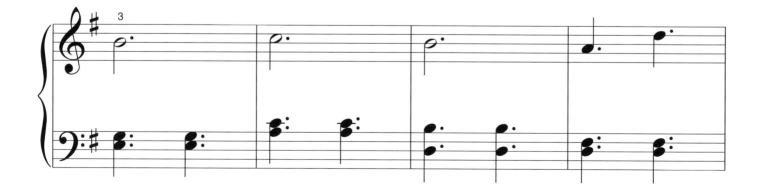

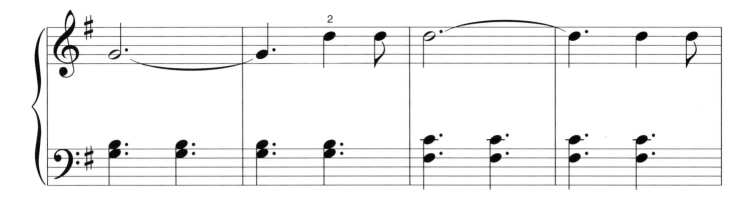

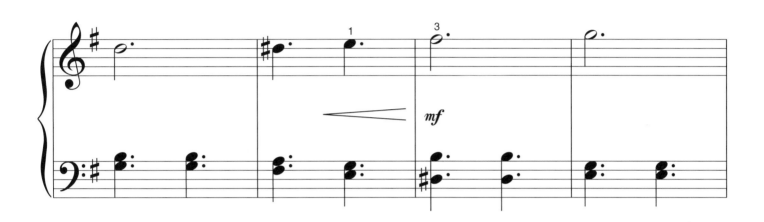

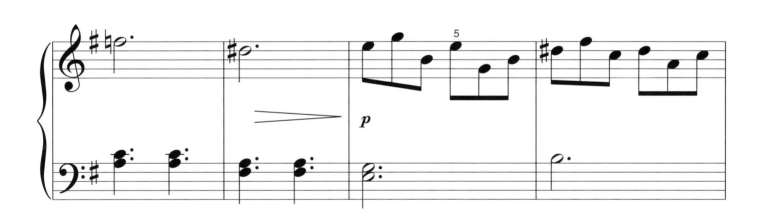

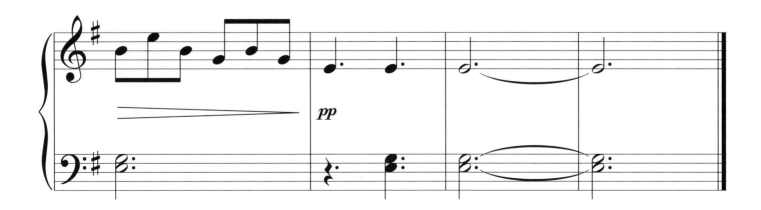

RUSSIAN FOLK SONG

By LUDWIG VAN BEETHOVEN

Con spirito

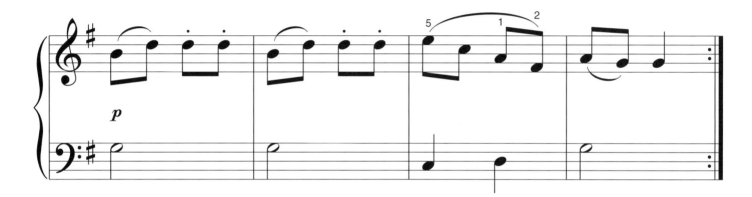

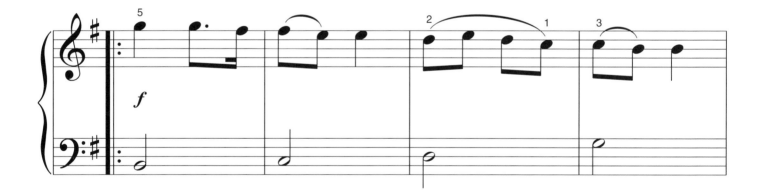

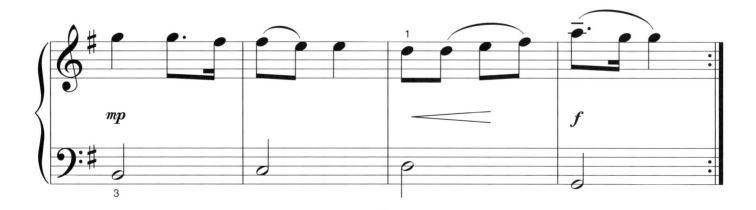

SYMPHONY NO. 5 IN C MINOR
First Movement Excerpt

By LUDWIG VAN BEETHOVEN

Allegro con brio

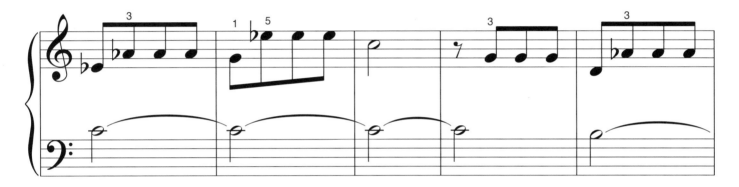

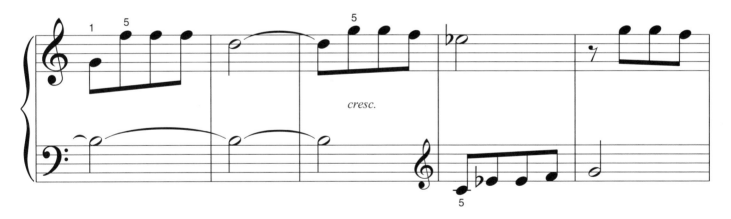

SYMPHONY NO. 6 IN F MAJOR
("PASTORAL")
First Movement Excerpt

By LUDWIG VAN BEETHOVEN

Allegro ma non troppo

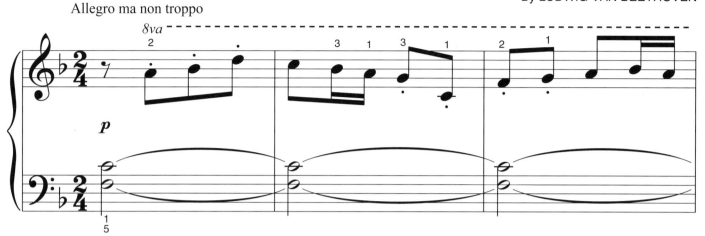

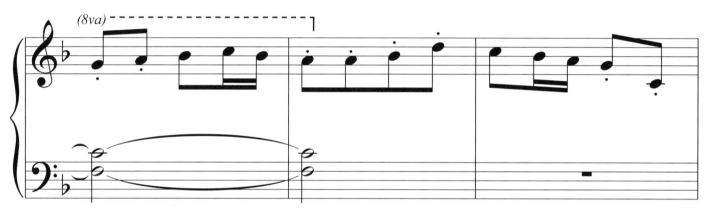

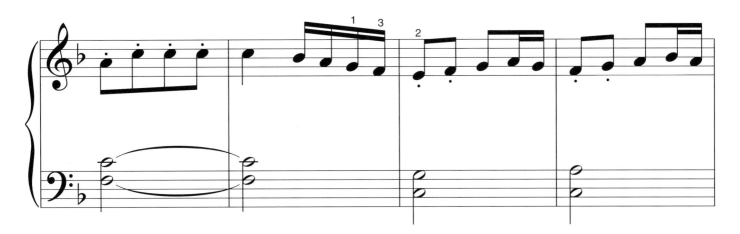

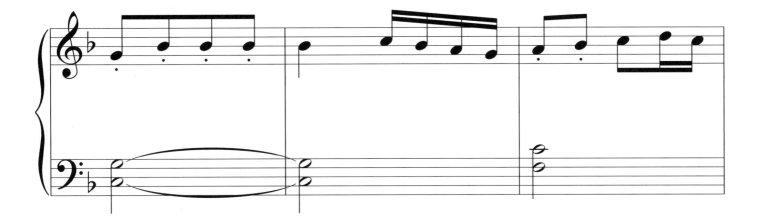

TURKISH MARCH
from THE RUINS OF ATHENS

By LUDWIG VAN BEETHOVEN

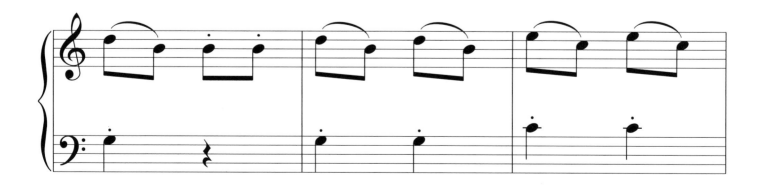

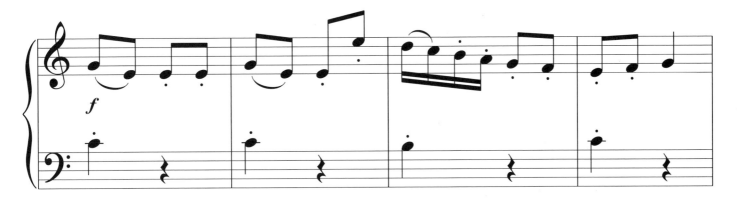

SYMPHONY NO. 7 IN A MAJOR
(Second Movement Theme)

By LUDWIG VAN BEETHOVEN